Why this [book has] been sent [to you]

If this country were ever at war the target of the enemy's bombers would be the staunchness of the people at home. We all hope and work to prevent war but, while there is risk of it, we cannot afford to neglect the duty of preparing ourselves and the country for such an emergency. This book is being sent out to help each householder to realise what he can do, if the need arises, to make his home and his household more safe against air attack.

The Home Office is working with the local authorities in preparing schemes for the protection of the civil population during an attack. But it is impossible to devise a scheme that will cover everybody unless each home and family play their part in doing what they can for themselves. In this duty to themselves they must count upon the help and advice of those who have undertaken the duty of advice and instruction.

If the emergency comes the country will look for her safety not only to her sailors and soldiers and airmen, but also to the organised courage and foresight of every household. It is for the volunteers in the air raid precautions services to help every household for this purpose, and in sending out this book I ask for their help.

Samuel Hoare

CONTENTS

THINGS TO DO NOW

On board ship, both crew and passengers are instructed where to go and what to do, not when danger threatens, but beforehand. The captain considers it a matter of ordinary routine and everyday precaution that everything is in readiness for a shipwreck which he hopes will never happen. If the head of the house will consider himself as " the captain of the ship " and put these air raid precautions into effect, the principal object of this book will have been achieved.

IF air raids ever came to this country, every home should have a refuge specially prepared in which the whole household could take cover. Every shop and office, or other place of work or business, would require a place similarly prepared for those engaged on the premises.

Every householder, or head of a family or business, should learn now how to protect, in war-time, his own people and home from the effects of explosive bombs, incendiary bombs, and poison gas. *This applies chiefly to those who live in large centres of population. In more remote districts the dangers would no doubt be less, though the need for protection and precautions would still exist.*

All the precautions recommended in this book are useful. Most of them can be adopted to some extent by everyone. The essential things cost little to do, and some of the more elaborate ones you will find you can do quite easily, either yourself or by combining with a neighbour, if you decide to begin NOW, and take your time.

Do not hesitate to ask for advice if you need it. A local air raid precautions organisation has been established in your district and air raid wardens have been appointed to help you. For any help you need, apply to your warden or to your local Council Offices.

WHAT TO DO NOW

The whole of this book is concerned with how to counter the danger of air attack. It is divided into sections so that you can turn quickly to any part and find out exactly what to do in any emergency. So please keep it carefully. But first read it through. Then come back to this page and think over these things.

1 Decide, according to the instructions given on page 8, what place would make the best refuge-room for your household at home, and begin to plan now how you would get it ready

2 If you are in charge of a business or shop, or an hotel or lodging house, or of tenements, decide upon places of refuge for those for whose safety and welfare you would be responsible.

3 Study carefully the precautions you can take against fire, and especially the instructions for dealing with a small incendiary bomb.

4 In time of war all buildings will have to be completely darkened at night. Be ready to do this for your home and any other premises for which you are responsible.

5 *Begin* to collect :—
>   materials for gas-protecting your refuge-room ;
>   materials for darkening your whole house or business premises ;
>   the things you would need in your refuge-room ;
>   simple fire appliances, if you can afford them.

6 If you live in a large town, think whether you can make arrangements for children, invalids and elderly persons, and pets, to be sent away the moment danger threatens, so that they may be in a place of greater safety.

7 Find out from your warden or local Council Offices the air raid precautions organisation and the emergency fire brigade arrangements being prepared in your district. As soon as you can get the information, fill in the spaces provided on the inside of the front cover of this book.

> *Most important of all, see that all grown-ups are familiar with the contents of this book and know of the arrangements you are making for their safety. Do not do nothing, either on the ground that there is no need, or because you think that nothing you can do will be of any avail. Your safety, and the safety of those for whom you are responsible, may depend on you.*

Darkening the house at night

It is vital that raiders should not see any lights at night; so vital that the Government might order the darkening of all buildings even before war broke out. So you must be ready to darken every window, skylight, glass door or exterior opening in parts of the house where lights are used after dark. You will need dark blinds, thick curtains, or some heavy material that will cover the windows completely. Material which lets anyone outside see that there is a light inside will not do. Bear this in mind when you next buy blinds and curtains. Skylights, fanlights and glass doors can best be covered with black paint or thick paper. If necessary get these things now, because in an emergency the shops might be quickly sold out.

RESPIRATORS

The Government is making arrangements to provide respirators free to the civilian population. But regard your respirator as your *second line* of defence and the precautions advised in this book as your *first*.

Your respirator will be kept safely stored, ready to be distributed very quickly if ever war is expected. You will be shown how to put one on so that you can get used to wearing it beforehand. Children can wear respirators. For those too young to wear them a special means of protection will be provided. A respirator is not uncomfortable to wear, and you can see and hear and speak when wearing it.

What a respirator is

A respirator consists of a rubber facepiece with a transparent window, and a container which holds the gas filters. If properly put on, it protects the eyes, nose, mouth and lungs; and ensures a supply of *pure* air for breathing, by means of filters which are able to absorb any gas known to be capable of being used in war. It has been designed for you by Government experts and, though simple to look at, exhaustive tests have shown it to be highly efficient. The facepiece, the edges of which fit closely round the face, prevents any air from getting inside the respirator except that which passes through the filters. It is held in position by adjustable straps behind the head. Once these straps have been properly adjusted, the respirator, if needed, can be put on instantly.

These war respirators do not afford protection against ordinary domestic coal gas or carbon monoxide, which cannot be used as war gases.

How to take care of your respirator

If your respirator is ever issued to you, take great care of it, and when not in use always keep it in its box, in a cool place.

After use, wipe off any moisture, either inside or outside, with a soft cloth and let the respirator dry before putting it away (but do not dry it in the sun or by artificial heat).

When not wearing the respirator, remember these rules :—

1. Do *not* expose it to strong light or heat.
2. Do *not* let it get wet.
3. Do *not* scratch or bend the window.
4. Do *not* carry or hang the respirator by the straps.

To stop the window clouding when you wear the respirator, rub your finger on a piece of wet soap (*not* carbolic), and apply a thin, even film of soap over the inside of the window.

Why a respirator alone is not enough

Your refuge-room is your first line of defence because a respirator cannot protect the other parts of your body from dangerous liquids, such as " mustard gas." These liquid " gases " need the most rigorous precautions, because they continue to be dangerous long after they have been dropped. The vapour as well as the liquid affects the skin of parts of the body not protected by the respirator. Remember, too, that by staying in a refuge-room you have some protection against flying splinters and debris, as well as additional protection against gas.

HOW TO CHOOSE A REFUGE-ROOM

Almost any room will serve as a refuge-room if it is soundly constructed, and if it is easy to reach and to get out of. Its windows should be as few and small as possible, preferably facing a building or blank wall, or a narrow street. If a ground floor room facing a wide street or a stretch of level open ground is chosen, the windows should if possible be specially protected (see pages 30 and 31). The stronger the walls, floor, and ceiling are, the better. Brick partition walls are better than lath and plaster, a concrete ceiling is better than a wooden one. An internal passage will form a very good refuge-room if it can be closed at both ends.

The best floor for a refuge-room

A cellar or basement is the best place for a refuge-room if it can be made reasonably gas-proof and if there is no likelihood of its becoming flooded by a neighbouring river that may burst its banks, or by a burst water-main. If you have any doubt about the risk of flooding ask for advice from your local Council Offices.

A cellar or basement is the best position for a refuge-room if it can be made reasonably gas-proof

Alternatively, any room on any floor below the top floor may be used. Top floors and attics should be avoided as they usually do not give sufficient protection overhead from small incendiary bombs. These small bombs would probably penetrate the roof but be stopped by the top floor, though they might burn through to the floor below if not quickly dealt with.

In a house with only two floors and without a cellar, choose a room on the ground floor so that you have protection overhead

In flats or tenement houses, either each household can make its own arrangements or communal refuges can be made. It is, however, important that top-floor dwellers should find accommodation downstairs. They might share a refuge-room, or they might make arrangements to occupy the basement. But the basement premises will have to be prepared as refuges in the same way as ordinary rooms, according to the instructions given in this book.

It is suggested that in any flats, or tenement house, or house occupied by more than one family, representa-

In a two-storeyed terrace house choose a room on the ground floor. The flanking walls will protect you from the blast of a bursting bomb

tives be chosen and formed into a Protection Committee to decide upon the most suitable rooms and to prepare them as refuge-rooms if it should ever be necessary for the safety of all.

Even though your household occupies one room only, many of the precautions recommended in the book can still be carried out, and will help to protect you. So do what you can.

How large should a refuge-room be ?

Although an actual raid may be over in a few minutes it might be necessary to stay in your refuge-room for some time, even perhaps for several hours, until the gas in the neighbourhood has been cleared away. You should therefore know how many persons can remain safely in one room without suffering any ill effects. For rooms of normal height (8 to 10 feet) an allowance of 20 square feet of floor area for each person will enable those persons to remain in the room with complete safety for a continuous period of twelve hours *without ventilation.*

A room 10 ft. × 10 ft. will hold 5 persons.
A room 15 ft. × 10 ft. will hold 7 persons.
A room 20 ft. × 12 ft. will hold 12 persons.

IF YOU CANNOT SPECIALLY SET ASIDE A ROOM FOR A REFUGE-ROOM

You can still make a refuge-room even if you have no surplus room to set aside, in war-time, specially for the purpose. If you have only one room you can make it a place of greater safety—even if you adopt only some of the suggestions contained in this book. Do not think you have no protection. Any room within solid walls is safer than being out in the open, so don't run out into the street to find better shelter if you ever get an air raid warning.

GET THESE THINGS FOR THE REFUGE-ROOM

These are some of the things that will be useful in your refuge-room. Keep them in mind and begin collecting those things you haven't got, one by one. Put them in a box, or in a drawer, in the room you have chosen for your refuge-room.

Things you probably possess already

Candles and matches	Old newspaper and brown paper
Hammer and nails	Some clean rags
Scissors	Needles, cotton, and thread

Things to collect

A candle lamp, or an electric hand lamp

Suitable material (see page 16) to protect the windows from the blast of an explosion

Gummed paper and adhesive tape

Plywood for blocking the fireplace : see page 14

A few tins or jars with air-tight lids for storing food

A bottle of disinfectant

A box of First Aid Supplies : see page 32

A list of *additional* things to get into your refuge-room, if there should ever be a war, is given on page 18.

If you have a wireless set or receiver it would be useful to have it in the refuge-room so that you could hear the news and pass the time away. Make sure that the plug for it, and the leads for the aerial and earth, if these are required, are made ready.

SECTION 2

THINGS TO DO IF
THERE SHOULD EVER
BE A WAR

*The Government will tell you when,
if ever, you should take the precautions recommended in this section.
There is no need to do any of
these things now, but read through
these notes carefully, bearing in
mind that they are intended to be
nothing more than notes. Think
them out, and see how to apply
them to your own home. You
will know, then, more exactly what
to do if there should ever be a war.
Having faced the problem before
danger threatens you will have
your plans made, and be ready to
carry them out quickly if ever
there is need.*

IFever you receive warning that war threatens, do these things at once :—

1 *Prepare and equip your refuge-room* (pages 13–18).

2 *Make all preparations for darkening the house at night. Windows, skylights, fanlights, glazed doors must be completely obscured* (see below).

3 *Clear the loft, attic, top floor, of inflammable stuff that can be moved, to lessen the risk of fire from an incendiary bomb that might penetrate the roof. Assemble appliances to fight fires. Also, if possible, limewash the timbers in the attic or roof space, and protect the floor* (page 19).

4 *If you live in a large town, children, invalids, elderly members of the household, and pets, should be sent to relatives or friends in the country, if this is possible.*

DARKEN YOUR HOUSE AT NIGHT

All windows, skylights, fanlights, glazed doors, or other openings in parts of the house where lights are used, must be completely screened after dusk, so that no light is visible from outside.

If blinds are used alone, they must be of stout material and dark in colour and must cover the window completely. If curtains are used they must be dark and thick. Dark blankets or carpets or thick sheets of brown paper can be used to cover windows temporarily.

Special care must be taken to cover completely skylights and other windows directly visible from the air.

All lights near an outside door must be screened so that no light can be seen when the door is opened. Outside lights, garden and porch lights, must not be used. If they are electric, take the bulbs out altogether.

HOW TO PREPARE YOUR REFUGE-ROOM
against the entry of gas

No serious amount of gas will come into a room unless there are draughts or currents of air to carry it in, so any cracks or openings must be sealed up somehow.

How to deal with cracks in walls, floors, and odd places

In old houses especially, windows and doors may shut badly. There may be chinks underneath the window sills on the inside. There may be cracks in the ceiling. The illustration below shows you the kind of places to look for. If possible make good these faults now without waiting for a war emergency.

Fill in all cracks and crevices with putty or a pulp made of sodden newspaper. Paste paper over any cracks in the walls or ceiling. Fill in the cracks between the floor boards and paste sheets of paper over the whole floor. If you have linoleum or an all-over carpet, it should be replaced after the cracks underneath have been filled up. Fill in all cracks round the skirting boards, or where pipes pass through the walls. All trap-doors, skylights and

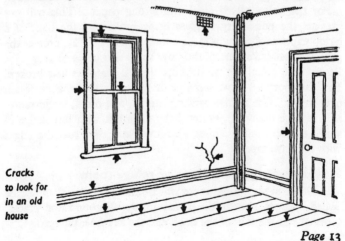

Cracks to look for in an old house

hatches in the room should be sealed, and interior ventilators stopped up with rags or pasted over with thick paper.

All ventilators in the outside walls of the house, including those below the floor level, should be stopped up with rags or paper.

If there is a fire-place, stuff the chimney with paper, rags, or sacks. Do not, of course, light a fire in the grate afterwards. Seal the front of the fire-place with a sheet of plywood and adhesive tape.

Plug key-holes. Plug waste-pipes, or overflow pipes, in any basin or sink in your refuge-room. If you are doubtful whether a hole or a crack lets in air, play for safety, and seal it up.

You can still use the room, for ordinary living purposes, provided you can do without a fire. If a fire is necessary, be ready to put it out quickly, and to seal the chimney and fire-place.

How to seal the windows of your refuge-room

The windows should be sealed so that draughts, or gas, cannot come in. Wedge them firmly to keep them tightly fixed in their frames. Seal all round the frames with gummed strip or pasted paper, wherever there is a crack. Be cautious, and make a thorough job of it. Any broken panes should be boarded in, or the holes pasted over with strong paper. This will not prevent the possibility of glass being broken by the blast of a bomb explosion, perhaps quite a long way away. So protect the glass if possible, in one of the ways suggested on page 16.

Be ready to reseal the window openings if the glass gets broken. For this purpose have some stout materials to hang or fasten over them. Use a close-woven material, or a blind, for instance, if it is large enough. Fasten it by nailing it with thin strips of wood to the window frame all round, and then seal the edges with adhesive tape.

How to seal the doors in your refuge-room

Doors to the refuge-room which need not be used should be sealed. Paper should be pasted firmly all round the cracks, especially at the foot of the door, and the key-hole plugged.

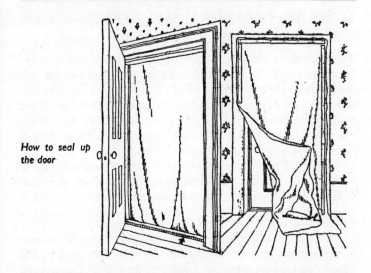

How to seal up
the door

Doors which have to be opened and closed should be sealed against gas. This is how to do it.

Nail a piece of wood, padded with felt, to the floor so that the door, when closed, presses tightly against it. Take care not to nail this piece of wood on the wrong side of the door so that it cannot be opened. Strips of felt may also be nailed round the inside of the door to exclude draughts. Fix a blanket outside the door if the door opens inwards, or inside the door if the door opens outwards, with strips of wood. The top of the blanket should be fixed to the top of the door frame. One side of the blanket should be fastened down the whole length of the door frame, on the side where the hinges are, by means of a strip of wood nailed to the frame. The other side of the blanket should be secured not more than two feet down, so that a flap is left free for going in and out. Arrange the blanket so that at least 12 inches trails on the floor to stop air from blowing underneath it. See illustration above. If the blanket is kept damp during an air raid, it will give better protection.

HOW TO PREPARE YOUR REFUGE-ROOM
against the effect of explosive bombs

There are three main types of bomb, an explosive bomb, an incendiary bomb, a gas bomb. Precautions against fire are described on page 19 and the way to deal with incendiary bombs and fires generally on pages 26 and 27, under the heading " What to do if fire breaks out." How to protect yourself against gas has already been explained. How to provide some protection against explosive bombs is dealt with here.

The essential thing is to protect your refuge-room against the shock of a bomb that may burst some distance away, and from flying glass and splinters caused by the explosion.

Protecting the windows of the refuge-room

Unless a window is barricaded with sandbags it is not easy to prevent the glass of closed windows being shattered by the blast of an explosion, even at some distance away. But you can prevent splinters of glass being blown into the room by covering the inside of the window panes with at least two thin sheets of one of the transparent or translucent, non-inflammable materials now commonly used for wrapping purposes and sold by stationers. The material must be tough and not readily torn. Although a cellulose varnish is the best adhesive, water glass or even ordinary gum can be used to stick the material to the glass, but examine it from time to time and regum when necessary.

Thin celluloid makes a better job, but a non-inflammable variety should be used, and it requires a cellulose varnish to stick it to the window pane. The moisture-proof variety of transparent wrapping material, such as is used on food packets and so on, also requires a cellulose varnish as an adhesive.

Failing anything better, some fabric material such as linen from old pillow cases, or mosquito netting, or even stout paper, may be pasted on the inside of the glass ; but these materials are not so effective as transparent wrapping material, or celluloid ; and they reduce the light.

Strengthening the room

If your refuge-room is on the ground floor or in the basement, you can support the ceiling with wooden props as an additional protection. The illustration shows a way of doing this, but it would be best to take a builder's advice before setting to work. Stout posts or scaffold poles are placed upright, resting on a thick plank on the floor and supporting a stout piece of timber against the ceiling, at right angles to the ceiling joists, i.e. in the same direction as the floor boards above.

How to support a ceiling

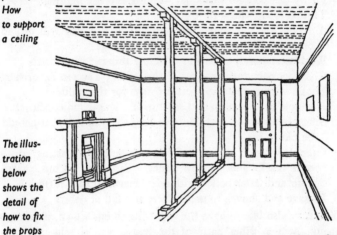

The illustration below shows the detail of how to fix the props

The smaller illustration shows how the posts are held in position at the top by two blocks of wood on the ceiling beam. The posts are forced tight by two wedges at the foot, driven in opposite ways. Do not drive these wedges too violently, otherwise you may lift the ceiling and damage it. If the floor of your refuge-room is solid, such as you might find in a basement, you will not need a plank across the whole floor, but only a piece of wood a foot or so long under each prop.

THINGS TO HAVE IN YOUR REFUGE-ROOM

Get these additional things into your refuge-room, as soon as the Government warns you of a threat of war, as well as the things listed on pages 10 and 32.

> A roll-call list of all who should be present. This applies particularly to business premises, or if the refuge-room is to be shared by neighbours
>
> Tables and chairs ; plates, cups, knives, forks, etc.
>
> Plenty of water for drinking, washing and fire fighting
>
> Tinned food, with a tin-opener
>
> A food chest of some kind (airtight tins or jars will do) to protect other food against contact with gas
>
> Washhand-stand, or basin ; washing things, soap, towels
>
> Chamber pots, toilet-paper ; disinfectant ; a screen for privacy
>
> Books, writing materials, cards ; toys for the children
>
> A simple hand-pump, and sand with a long-handled shovel
>
> Spare blankets or rugs for resealing the window if it should be blown in
>
> Gummed paper, or pots of paste or gum, for pasting paper over cracks and window panes. Paste can be made from flour and water boiled with a few cloves to keep it fresh
>
> Pickaxe and shovel, to use if there is a fall of debris

You may also like to have the following things which, if you are using them in other parts of the house, you should take into your refuge-room when you hear the air raid warning.

> A mattress, or mattresses, to lie on
>
> Overcoats, blankets, eiderdowns, rugs and warm coverings
>
> The wireless set, gramophone with records
>
> Mackintoshes, goloshes, gum boots

An electric kettle is useful if you have one, but don't burn a gas fire or gas ring, as it uses up air.

If the weather is really cold, you may use an electric fire in your refuge-room for a while if you wish. But the air will remain much fresher if you can avoid artificial heating of any kind. It is better to rely on coats and blankets for warmth.

PRECAUTIONS AGAINST FIRE

An air attack may include the use of large numbers of small incendiary bombs. So many fires might be started that the fire brigades could not deal with them, and every citizen must be prepared to help. Do these things the moment you receive official warning that war threatens.

1 Make sure that you know the emergency fire brigade arrangements in your neighbourhood—whether fire patrols have been established and where the nearest fire station is.

2 Clear the loft, attic, or top floor of all inflammable material, paper, litter, lumber, etc., to lessen the danger of fire, and to prevent fire from spreading.

3 If the materials are available, protect the floor of the loft, attic, or top floor in one of the following ways—with sheets of corrugated iron or plain sheet iron (gauge 22 or thicker) or asbestos wallboard, or with 2 inches of sand (if the floor will bear the weight).

4 It is advisable to coat all woodwork in the attic or roof space with limewash, to delay its catching fire. A suitable mixture is 2 lb. of slaked lime and 1 oz. of common salt with 1 pint of *cold* water. Apply 2 coats.

5 For controlling an incendiary bomb (see page 27), have on an upper floor a bucket or box of dry sand or earth with a shovel fitted with a long handle. Better still, have a Redhill sand container (Home Office Specification). It has a suitable scoop and hoe and is strong enough to hold a small incendiary bomb without risk of burning through.

6 Water is the best means of putting out a fire, but water mains may be damaged in an air raid or the flow restricted by fire fighting operations, so make sure that you have some water ready in buckets or cans in get-at-able places about the house.

The water is more effective if applied through a jet with force behind it. A simple appliance for household use is the Stirrup Hand Pump (Home Office Specification) for use with an ordinary bucket. It has 30 feet of hose and a special nozzle which can be adjusted to deliver a jet for dealing with fires or a spray for use on an incendiary bomb (see page 27). Because of its two uses, it is more generally useful than the Redhill sand container. But remember that water must *not* be thrown on an incendiary bomb except as spray.

PUBLIC WARNING SIGNALS

The *Air Raid Warning* may be given by hooters or sirens, and will be either a continuous, fluctuating note, or a succession of blasts with silent intervals between. The whole signal will last two minutes. (In addition, the police and wardens may blow sharp blasts on their whistles.)

The *Raiders Passed Signal* will be a continuous signal at a steady pitch, also lasting two minutes.

The Air Raid Warning *means that raiders may reach your district in about five minutes. This does not necessarily mean that they will drop bombs near you : they may go farther on. So that, though you should take all precautions, you are not necessarily in danger.*

The Raiders Passed Signal *means that the raiders have left the district. But there may be gas about, so take care when coming out of your refuge-room.*

Street Signals

A *local Gas Warning* will be given when gas has been dropped. Wardens will give it by means of a *hand rattle* in the streets affected.

The ringing of *handbells*, after the *Raiders Passed Signal*, will mean either that no gas is present or that there is no further danger from gas.

SECTION 3

THINGS TO DO
IN AN AIR RAID

*This section describes the ACTION
you would need to take during a
war, as soon as you received warning of the actual approach of hostile
aircraft. Only at such a time will
the value of the previous sections
become fully apparent.*

*The head of the house takes com-
mand, and because everyone in the
household knows what to do and
where to go, there is no indecision
and no panic. Risk is reduced
to a minimum. Appointed tasks
are undertaken, appointed places
" manned " without hesitation and
without confusion.*

IMMEDIATELY ON HEARING THE WARNING AS HEAD OF THE HOUSEHOLD YOU SHOULD . . .

Personally supervise the following precautions—

1 Send every member of the household immediately to the refuge-room, *making certain that each person has a respirator.*

Pets should, if possible, have been sent away into the country at the first sign of danger. But if they are still in the house they should be taken into the refuge-room, otherwise they may come into contact with gas, or get splashed by it, and contaminate you. But it should be remembered that animals will help to use up the supply of air in the room. To be on the safe side, count two dogs or cats as one person in choosing the size of your refuge-room.

2 Make some other member of the family, previously appointed for the purpose, responsible for checking that all the articles needed for the refuge-room are properly in place (see lists on pages 10, 18 and 32), and that the room is properly sealed up against gas, the fire put out, and the chimney blocked up. The blanket over the door should be made damp.

3 Go all round the house, closing all doors and all windows, to reduce the amount of gas which can get into any part of the house.

4 After dark, see that no lights are left burning that may be visible from outside.

5 Extinguish all fires in grates. Fires cause currents of air which may draw in gas from outside. Do not put out these fires with water, as this will fill the house with irritant fumes. Smother them with earth or sand or salt.

6 If you have electric light you may use it, but all gas points that are burning should be turned off. It is better to turn off the gas at the meter, in case the pipes in the house got damaged and began to leak. Do not use gas light or paraffin lamps in the refuge-room, and if you use candles do not burn more at a time than is necessary, to avoid using up oxygen. If the passages to the refuge-room are very dark, you may light them with candles.

7 See that the water buckets or cans which you will have placed about the house are full and ready for use.

This information is given to guide you. Your own common-sense will tell you of other things to do, according to the position of your refuge-room and the type of house you live in.

When these duties have been seen to, the head of the house or other responsible person should go to the refuge-room, and after making certain that EVERYONE IS THERE SHOULD CLOSE THE DOOR AND SEE THAT THE SEALING ARRANGEMENTS ARE EVERYWHERE INTACT.

If the house is a large one, it would be a good thing for someone to stay outside the refuge-room, on an upper floor or in a trench or dug-out outside, as a watcher in case an incendiary bomb falls on the house or on a neighbouring building. This is not necessary in small houses. The watcher should carry his respirator ready for instant use.

WHAT TO DO IN YOUR REFUGE-ROOM

These rules should be closely observed by all persons sheltering in a refuge-room.

1 Sit, or preferably lie down, and keep still, keeping warm with blankets or other coverings.

2 Don't smoke.

3 Don't light fires.

4 Don't go out, unless you must, until you hear the " Raiders Passed " signal. Be very cautious even then. The danger of gas may not be over although the air raid may have ended. Only one member of the household should go out first to investigate, and he should be wearing his respirator.

5 Pass the time reading, writing, sewing, playing cards or quiet games, listening to the wireless or gramophone. Avoid exertion. Don't let the children romp about as they will only tire themselves out and get exhausted.

6 Do not put on your respirator unless the room is damaged, unless you have to go out, unless you actually smell gas. Remember, too, that a respirator affords no protection against ordinary coal gas.

7 Do not eat food that has come into contact with gas. A food-chest of some kind, or air-tight jars and tins, will guard against this danger.

> *Don't forget, on coming out of your refuge-room, that whether the raid is over or not, you may find the rest of the house full of gas. So, except in emergency, keep your family in the refuge-room until you are sure the house is free of gas, or until it has been cleared.*

WHAT TO DO IF THE HOUSE IS DAMAGED

At once put on your respirator. If you have to go out of your refuge-room, seek refuge in another room or in another building. If you have to go out of doors keep on your respirator, and wear a mackintosh and goloshes or gum boots if you have them. Avoid all damp splashes on the ground that might be gas. If anyone is injured, a message should be sent to the warden's post, or the nearest first aid party or post. Until help comes act according to the instructions in Section 5, at the end of the book.

HOW TO AVOID INJURY FROM MUSTARD GAS

Mustard gas, whether in the form of liquid or of the vapour which the liquid gives off, will injure any part of the body with which it comes in contact. It also " contaminates " clothing, or other objects exposed to it, making them dangerous to have near you or to touch until they have been " decontaminated." If you have come in contact with the liquid or vapour of mustard change all your clothing as soon as possible, put it right outside the house, and wash yourself thoroughly with soap and water. Your shoes should be taken off before entering the house and left outside. Any outer garment which has actually touched liquid gas should be taken off *immediately*.

To be of use, the washing and changing must be done within twenty minutes at the outside. Take these precautions yourself if you can take them quickly ; if not, go to the nearest first aid post.

If liquid gas has been in contact with your skin, wash that part of yourself *immediately* with soap and water, then change and wash as described above. If you cannot take these measures *at once*, go to the nearest first aid post straight away.

If you have been actually splashed with liquid gas or have passed through an area which has been splashed with it, go to a first aid post for further treatment after taking the precautions described above.

WHAT TO DO IF FIRE BREAKS OUT

1 Do your best to put the fire out **yourself.**
2 If you cannot do so, summon help at once by calling a fire patrol, air raid warden, or policeman. Have someone on the look-out so that when helpers arrive, you can show them at once where to get to work.
3 See to the safety of all those in the house. If the refuge-room is in danger, get the occupants out. See that they have their respirators on and know what to do.
4 If the gas pipes in the house are damaged, turn the gas supply off at the main, if this has not been done already.

General guidance for dealing with fires

Any ordinary fire can be put out with water, which should be applied, with force, at the seat of the fire. A fire resulting from an incendiary or explosive bomb is like an ordinary fire. It is only the incendiary bomb itself which requires special treatment. This is described on the opposite page.

Keep in mind the following rules.

Close *all* doors and windows and keep them closed. If room doors are left open the staircase will act as a flue and the fire will quickly spread. A closed door will confine the fire for a time.

If you have to open a door which may have fire on the other side, and it opens towards you, place your foot a few inches from it before turning the handle. The door may fly open, but your foot will check it. The door will protect you against smoke, flame and hot gases, and you can shut it again if necessary. By keeping close to a wall, it is often possible to move quite safely about a room or a corridor or down a staircase which has been weakened by the effect of fire.

When you have to go near the seat of a fire, keep low and crawl if necessary, because the smoke and fumes are much less thick near the floor.

If a person's clothes catch fire, roll him on the ground, preferably in a rug or blanket.

How to deal with an incendiary bomb

You can tackle a small incendiary bomb yourself (better if you have someone to help you) if you will follow these directions. You will also be able to get proper instruction about it.

The bomb will burn fiercely for a minute or so, throwing out burning sparks, and afterwards less fiercely. It will set fire to anything inflammable within reach. You should try to deal with it before it has caused a big fire.

Before you can get close enough to do anything, you will probably have to cool down the room with water, preferably with a line of hose. (See page 20 for a simple hand pump.)

There are two ways of dealing with the bomb itself.

1 It can be controlled by means of the Stirrup Hand Pump (see page 20), with a *spray* of water which, although it does not extinguish the bomb, makes it burn out quickly and helps to prevent the fire spreading. Water must *not* be used on a bomb in any other way.

2 If it has fallen where you can get at it, it can be smothered with dry sand or earth. A bucket full of sand or earth is enough to cover and control a small bomb. The best method of applying it is by the Redhill sand container and scoop (see page 19); but a bucket will do if you have a long-handled shovel to use with it.

Immediately the bomb is smothered, shovel or scoop it into the sand container or bucket and take it out of doors. If a bucket is used, 2 or 3 inches of sand or earth must be kept in the bottom to prevent the bomb burning through.

Remember that the bomb might burn through the floor before you have had time to remove it, and you might have to continue to deal with it on the floor below.

ACT PROMPTLY. PROMPT ACTION MAY BE THE MEANS OF SAVING LIVES. PROMPT ACTION WILL SAVE PROPERTY. PROMPT ACTION WILL PREVENT SERIOUS DAMAGE. PROMPT ACTION WILL DEFEAT THE OBJECT OF THE RAID.

WHAT TO DO WHEN OUT OF DOORS

Always carry a respirator with you throughout the war

If you are out of doors at the time of an air raid, seek shelter at once. If it is impossible to get under cover it is safer to lie on the ground than to stand up, unless you stand in a doorway or narrow archway.

A limited number of public refuges will be available which will provide some protection for those caught in the streets.

Remember other people caught out of doors

If you have any space to spare in your refuge-room, and there is no special reason for not admitting strangers, be ready to take in someone who is caught in the street outside.

WHAT TO DO WHEN YOU COME OUT OF YOUR REFUGE-ROOM

Remember that gas may still be about after the " Raiders Passed " signal has been sounded.

If you detect gas in your house, keep your refuge-room closed up, but open all the other windows and doors. If you are in doubt, summon an air raid warden.

If you know bombs have fallen close by, go all round the house to see if any damage has been done. Look out of doors to see if your neighbours want any help.

If you have turned off the domestic gas supply at the main, inspect every gas point as soon as you turn it on again to make sure that no tap was left on or has been turned on accidentally.

Unexploded bombs

If you know of a bomb which has fallen but has not exploded, tell a policeman or air raid warden at once.

Leave it alone and keep away from it. It may still explode, even some time after it has been dropped. But this does not apply to a small incendiary bomb, which may be carefully picked up, if it is in a building or dangerous place, and carried in a bucket of water to a place of safety.

SECTION 4

EXTRA PRECAUTIONS

This section describes extra pre-cautions which it is useful to take if you can, as they provide an additional protection against the effect of explosive bombs and against the penetration of gas. But do not be worried if they are more than you are able to take. The simpler precautions described in Section 2 are the essential things to do.

A list is also given of simple first aid supplies, and space is provided in which you can note any other things which you may think it useful to get or do for your refuge-room.

EXTRA PRECAUTIONS AGAINST EXPLOSIVE BOMBS

TRENCHES. Instead of having a refuge-room in your house, you can, if you have a garden, build a dug-out or a trench. A trench provides excellent protection against the effects of a bursting bomb, and is simple to construct. Full instructions will be given in another book which you will be able to buy. Your air raid wardens will also be able to advise.

SANDBAGS. Sandbags outside are the best protection if your walls are not thick enough to resist splinters. Do not rely on a wall keeping out splinters unless it is more than a foot thick. Sandbags are also the best protection for window openings. If you can completely close the window opening with a wall of sandbags you will prevent the glass being broken by the blast of an explosion, as well as keeping out splinters. But the window must still be sealed inside against gas.

A basement window protected by boxes of earth

Any bags or sacks, including paper sacks such as are used for cement, will do for sandbags. But if they are large, don't fill them right up or you won't be able to carry them. If you cannot get sand, use earth instead. It will serve as well.

If you haven't got sandbags, a wall of boxes filled with earth will do instead. The box wall should not be less than 2 ft. 6 ins. thick. If the boxes are large, fill them in position. The boxes should be quite full and the earth well pressed down. If your refuge-room is in a basement, and the window opens on to an area which you cannot fill in or cover over, build a wall of sandbags or boxes of earth round the top of the cellar area. See illustration on page 30.

Save any small sacks or cloth bags or stout paper sacks you may get from time to time, even a few will be useful. Collect now wooden boxes or large cardboard cartons that will hold earth.

EXTRA PRECAUTIONS AGAINST GAS

You have been told how to seal your refuge-room against gas. Try also to keep gas out of the rest of the house by blocking up ventilators and cracks, as recommended for the refuge-room, and by protecting as many windows as possible against being broken by blast, as described on page 16. Then if you shut all windows and doors before a raid, there will be much less risk of gas penetrating into the house while you are in the refuge-room.

An additional precaution in flats or large buildings would be an air-lock at the door of a communal refuge-room, or at a main outer door, or in a corridor which had to be used frequently. An air-lock is simply two gas-proof doors or curtains 4 feet or more apart, with a space between them sealed like a refuge-room. Persons can then pass through without admitting gas, provided they close the first door or curtain when they are inside the air-lock before opening the second.

SIMPLE FIRST AID SUPPLIES

You should have, as suggested in the list on page 10, a few first aid supplies for your refuge-room. The list of articles below is about right for a household of six or seven persons all sheltering in one room. For hints on how to use them, see Section 5.

3 1-oz. packets of lint, for dressing wounds
3 1-oz. packets of cotton wool, for pads on dressings
2 triangular bandages, for use as arm-slings or, when folded, as bandages
3 1-in. roller bandages, for fingers
3 2½-in. roller bandages, for head or limbs
3 3-in. roller bandages, for limbs or body
1 dozen small safety pins
1 pair of scissors
1 bottle of smelling salts
Sal volatile
Iodine, or antiseptic

MAKE IN THE SPACE BELOW A LIST
**of any other things which occur to you as
worth getting or doing for your own refuge-room**

SECTION 5

WHAT TO DO
IF ANYONE IS HURT

If you carry out the precautions given in this book you will know that you have done everything you reasonably can to protect yourself and those dependent on you. It is possible, however, that someone in your household might be injured. That is why those who can should learn something about first aid.

Some general principles are given here, but a simple first aid training —which may prove useful to anyone in everyday life—may be had from the St. John Ambulance Brigade, the St. Andrew's Ambulance Association, or the British Red Cross Society. You can get information about the training available in your own locality from your local Council Offices.

A list of simple first aid supplies is given on the opposite page.

ALL persons involved in accidents suffer from shock, whether or not they suffer physical injury. Shock is a disturbance of the nervous system. It varies in its severity. The signs of shock are faintness, paleness, weak pulse, and weak breathing.

TREATMENT OF SHOCK

1 Place the patient flat on his back on a bed or a rug or on cushions. If you think a bone may be broken do not move the patient more than can be helped.

2 Loosen the clothing at the neck, chest and waist to make the breathing freer.

3 Cover the patient warmly with rugs and blankets. In cases of shock the body loses heat. A hot-water bottle is helpful, but take care that it does not lie in contact with the skin.

4 Give hot drinks. If you cannot make hot drinks, give cold water *in sips*. But only if the patient is conscious and able to swallow.

5 Soothe the patient by speaking reassuring words in a calm voice and in a confident way.

TREATMENT OF WOUNDS

The first thing to do is to stop the bleeding and to keep the wound clean. This can be done by covering it with a clean dressing bound on tightly. Do not touch a wound with your fingers because of the risk of poisoning from dirt. Treat the patient for shock in addition to attending to the wound, because the loss of blood, if the wound is serious, and the pain do in themselves cause shock.

WOUNDS IN THE HEAD AND BODY

1 Cover the wound with a clean folded handkerchief or a double layer of dry lint.

2 Apply another handkerchief or a layer of cotton wool as a pad to distribute the pressure over the wound.

3 Tie the dressing in position with a bandage, a strip of linen, or a necktie. This can be done quite firmly, unless there is any foreign body, especially glass, in the wound, or unless the bone is broken. In this case the dressing should be tied on lightly.

4 Treat the patient for shock.

WOUNDED LIMBS

1 First raise the limb to lessen the flow of blood.

2 If the flow of blood is steady (when a vein is injured) cover the wound with a dressing, and bandage it firmly as already described.

3 If the blood comes in spurts and the blood itself is brilliant red (when an artery is injured), raise the limb, and grasp it tightly between the wound and the point where the limb joins the body. Get someone else to apply dressings in the way already described. Keep the limb well raised. Release your grasp. Watch carefully. If the bleeding starts again, renew your grip and hold the limb firmly until skilled help arrives.

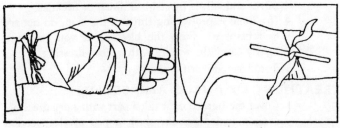

If it is too tiring to keep your grasp, tie the limb firmly with a bandage (or a tie or handkerchief or even stout string), insert a stick (or a large skewer, or spoon, or fork) in the knot as shown in the illustration, and twist it until the bleeding stops. Then tie the stick, or whatever you use, firmly in position.

If help does not come within about fifteen minutes, untwist the stick and loosen the bandage. If the bleeding starts again, the bandage and stick must again be tightened. Loosen them again at intervals of about fifteen minutes. When there is no further bleeding, the wound can be dressed in the ordinary way, but care must be taken not to move the limb.

4 Treat the patient for shock.

TREATMENT FOR BROKEN BONES

If bones or limbs are broken it is extremely unwise to move the patient more than is absolutely necessary. The patient often assumes by instinct a position in which the broken limb or bone is most comfortable. If you are doubtful whether a bone is broken, act as though it is, and do not move the patient unless you must.

1 Support the patient with cushions or folded blankets tucked closely round the body so that he can relax into the position he finds most comfortable.

2 A temporary arm-sling will sometimes relieve the pain of a broken arm.

3 A broken leg can sometimes be made more comfortable by being tied to the other leg at the thighs, calves and ankles by strips of linen or neckties.

4 If a bone is protruding through the skin, do not try to replace it. Stop the bleeding if you can, and lightly cover the wound with a clean dressing.

5 Treat the patient for shock.

TREATMENT OF BURNS AND SCALDS

1 Cover the burned or scalded part with a *dry* dressing, a clean folded handkerchief, a pad of clean cotton wool, or a piece of lint folded double. Do *not* apply oil or butter to the burn.

2 Treat the patient for shock.

TREATMENT FOR GAS

Many of the gases which might be used in war are not necessarily dangerous to life if proper care is taken.

Contaminated clothes should be removed (see page 25). The eyes should be freely washed out, the skin washed with soap and water, the throat and mouth gargled.

Until skilled assistance can be obtained, the patient must have absolute rest and quiet. He must not drink alcohol or smoke.

Keep calm and act quickly